1 MONTH OF
FREE
READING

at

www.ForgottenBooks.com

By purchasing this book you are eligible for one month membership to ForgottenBooks.com, giving you unlimited access to our entire collection of over 1,000,000 titles via our web site and mobile apps.

To claim your free month visit:

www.forgottenbooks.com/free1249906

ISBN 978-0-428-62365-4
PIBN 11249906

This book is a reproduction of an important historical work. Forgotten Books uses
state-of-the-art technology to digitally reconstruct the work, preserving the original format
whilst repairing imperfections present in the aged copy. In rare cases, an imperfection in
the original, such as a blemish or missing page, may be replicated in our edition. We do,
however, repair the vast majority of imperfections successfully; any imperfections that
remain are intentionally left to preserve the state of such historical works.

ates
ent of·
re

ral

Series

991

a H D 9 0 0 1
A 37
cz

AGRICULTURAL TRADE HIGHLIGHTS

s Fall for Fourth Month
'ear-ago Levels

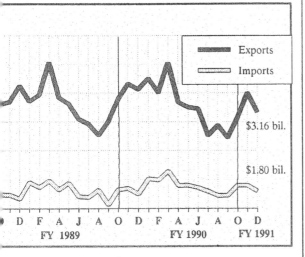

$3.16 bil.

$1.80 bil.

D F A J A O D F A J A O D
FY 1989   FY 1990   FY 1991

trade statistics released uary 15 by the Com- rtment revealed that ultural exports for the 1 $3.16 billion. This was illion from November's so down $400 million ber of last year. This month in a row that has dropped from year- Much of the decline is ontinued decline in the lk commodity exports , corn, and soybeans.

ort volume fell also. ports totaled 10.3 mil- 28 percent from a year as due primarily to exports which were off , or 45 percent.

led $1.8 billion, down from November but up from last December. ed with the export per-

formance, puts December's agricultural trade surplus at $1.36 billion.

Exports of high-value products continued to grow in December, but were more than offset by continuing declines in bulk commodity sales, echoing trends of the past few months. Among bulk products, wheat exports fell 51 percent and totaled only $179 million. This precipitous decline was due not only to lower prices, but also to a 31-percent fall in volume. Corn exports during December were off by almost half in both value and volume while soybeans were down 16 percent. Cotton and tobacco are the only bright spots among bulk commodities, with value increases of 13 percent and 71 percent, respectively.

High-value products appear to be headed for another record year with exports advancing over a broad range

of products. Gains were led by horticultural products (up 51 percent to $466 million), red meats (up 20 percent to $190 million), and poultry products (up 18 percent to $72 milion).

Export performance with our top 10 trading partners was mixed with 5 up and 5 down. Among those showing gains were the EC (up 7 percent), Japan (up 5 percent), Canada (up 75 percent, mainly due to changes in statistical reporting methods), Saudi Arabia (up 27 percent), and Hong Kong (up 25 percent). The markets that declined were led again this month by the Soviet Union (down 87 percent to $52 million). Others include Taiwan (down 41 percent), Egypt (down 22 percent), Korea (down 17 percent), and Mexico (down 4 percent).

Exports for the first quarter of fiscal 1991 reached a total of $9.7 billion, down 8 percent from the same period last year. Imports to date now total $5.6 billion, down 3 percent leaving the trade surplus at $4.15 billion, down $1 billion from the first quarter of fiscal 1990.

U.S. Agricultural Export Summaries
Fiscal Year Comparisons and Latest Month

Product Summary

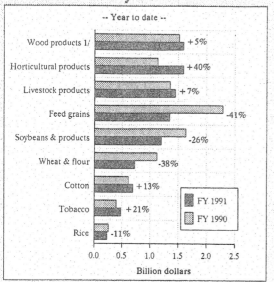

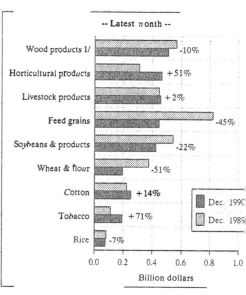

Top Ten Markets Summary

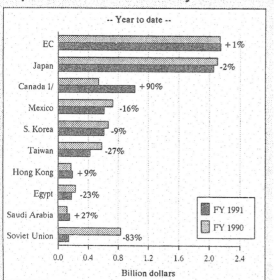

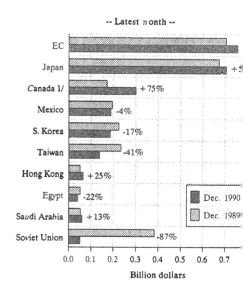

Note: Percentages are computed as the change from a year ago

1/ U.S. agricultural exports to Canada have been under-repo recognized by both Governments. Effective January 1990, t statistics to account for these differences.

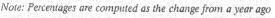

ts

respectively, the European
_pan at $706 million topped
s in December._ Both markets
_.ins, unmanufacurted tobacco,
However, these increases were
declines in wheat and flour
wn 41 percent), and soybeans
in an overall agricultural ex-
cember 1989._

The volume of _rice_ exports was up
12 percent in December while total
value was down 7 percent reflecting
lower prices this year. December's
sales brought exports to date to $236
million on shipments of 839,000 tons,
down 11 percent in value but up
4 percent in volume. Brazil, Saudi
Arabia, and the Ivory Coast all experienced substantial increases in export value for the first quarter of fiscal 1991. However, declines to
Mexico, the EC and Iraq were large
enough to cause overall export value
to fall during the 3-month period.

All _soybean product_ categories
soybeans, soybean oil, and soybean
meal--experienced significant
declines in December. This was also
seen for the first quarter of fiscal
1991, with total sales to date drop-
ping 26 percent to $1.21 billion. The
top three markets, the EC, Japan,
and Taiwan, all experienced significant declines. With prices roughly unchanged from last year, this
reduction was due to lower volume--
the result of lower foreign demand
and increased competition from Argentina.

Cotton exports in December continued to increase for the second
month, fueled by stronger exports to
Thailand, Mexico, and the EC. Total
exports in December reached
$284 million, a 13-percent increase
over last year. The cumulative-to-

date total for fiscal 1991 also increased 13 percent putting sales at
$693 million.

Sales of _unmanufactured tobacco_
continued to flourish in December,
gaining 71 percent to reach $193 mil-
lion. The first quarter totals reached
$481 million, a 21-percent gain over
fiscal 1990. The EC and Japan led
the growth with increases of 31 and
45 percent, respectively. Taiwan was
the only major market to register a
decline, falling 41 percent to $45 mil-
lion.

Livestock products advanced slightly
in December, increasing 3 percent to
$456 million. Beef and veal exports
were the main cause of this growth.
As a result, sales in the first 3 months
of fiscal 1991 posted a gain, increasing 7 percent to $1.45 billion. Japan
easily remained the largest market
for U.S. livestock products, followed
by the EC and Canada.

Horticultural products continued with
strong growth in December, increasing 51 percent to $465 million over
December 1989. Exports of fresh
deciduous fruits and fresh vegetables
led the growth increasing 59 percent
and 170 percent, respectively.
Canada, with a cumulative-to-date
increase of 154 percent to reach
$490 million, continues to be the
dominant market in fiscal 1991 followed by the EC and Japan. However, much of this increase is at-
tributable to changes in statistical
reporting methods to Canada.

Wood product sales in December
declined 10 percent to $507 million
over year-ago levels. However, first
quarter totals registered a gain of 5
percent. Japan, the EC, and Canada
continue to be the largest markets.

_For more information contact, Kelly
Kirby, (202) 382-1034._

Top Five Markets for Major U.S. Commodities
October - December Comparisons

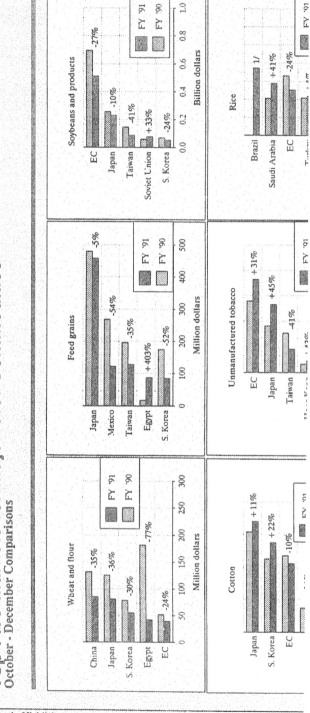

Wheat and flour (Million dollars)

	FY '91 / FY '90
China	-35%
Japan	-36%
S. Korea	-30%
Egypt	-77%
EC	-24%

Feed grains (Million dollars)

Japan	-5%
Mexico	-54%
Taiwan	-35%
Egypt	+403%
S. Korea	-52%

Soybeans and products (Billion dollars)

EC	-27%
Japan	-10%
Taiwan	-41%
Soviet Union	+33%
S. Korea	-24%

Cotton (Million dollars)

Japan	+11%
S. Korea	+22%
EC	-10%

Unmanufactured tobacco

EC	+31%
Japan	+45%
Taiwan	-41%

Rice

Brazil	1/
Saudi Arabia	+41%
EC	-24%

ɔne of the
est export
oducts. In
top three
U.S. farm
ears. This
ɟg by leaps
ast decade,
ultural im-
ord levels
ɔortantly,
ade by the
ating with
restrictive
stifled the
food sales
n the latter
the United
ɪnd increas-
is sure to
source of
lue agricul-

ɔlies Korea
ɔtal imports
record $6.3
ɔrts in fiscal
llion, up 10

percent from fiscal 1989, establishing Korea as the United States' fifth largest export market. Exports for fiscal 1991 are expected to be roughly unchanged from 1990. Both the value and volume of U.S. exports to Korea have shown impressive rates of growth over the last 5 years. Since 1985, both have almost doubled. Likewise, the overall size of the Korean import market has more than doubled since 1985 with total imports from the world valued at $3 billion jumping to $6.3 billion in 1989. While Korean imports of traditional bulk commodities, such as wheat, corn, and cotton, have risen 44 percent since 1985, imports of high-value products, such as intermediate and consumer-oriented food products, have shown even greater expansion, rising by 170 and 436 percent, respectively. Nonetheless, the import of bulk commodities continues to dominate, accounting for half of Korea's agricultural imports and over half of total U.S. exports to the country.

Korea's major agricultural imports, which are used as raw materials in the country's light industries, include animal hides and cotton. The importance of these commodities to Korea's export industries, specifically textiles and leather, helps assure the United States of a dependable market for as long as Korea is competitive in global markets. The other significant U.S. export to Korea is

corn. U.S. corn exports destined for the Korean livestock sector are expected to continue to do well since the sector is tied closely to the overall health of the economy. Given domestic grain production cannot keep pace with demand, Korea must import the majority of its feedstuffs. New markets for corn are developing in the food and processed food sectors as well. Strong growth occurred in these market segments during the last 2 years. When the values of corn, hides and skins, cotton, wheat, and soybeans are combined, the total amounted to 85 percent of total U.S. farm exports to Korea in 1990.

However, consumer-oriented high-value products may well offer the greatest potential and toughest challenge for U.S. exporters. The booming Korean economy has created a huge market in urban centers for high-value products such as fresh and processed fruits and vegetables, meats, and confectionary goods. This recent surge in demand is most likely to be met through a combination of a restructuring of Korean agriculture and increased imports. However, products in this sector have been affected by the "anti-import" movement, which opposes any imports that may be a threat to the "traditional" Korean society. In the past 2 years, Korea has increasingly used technical nontariff barriers in an attempt to curb the import of foreign high-value products.

Nonetheless, an opinion survey conducted by a Korean newspaper and Seoul National University found that the majority of the Korean population supports the liberalization of their markets. Approximately 65 percent of the country's 43 million population are 30 and younger and anxious to become international consumers. If policies succumb to the demands of the young consumers, the potential of Korea as an export market, particularly for high-value products, is unlimited.

For more information, contact Lori Huthoefer, (202) 382-9055

KOREAN BILATERAL TRADE RELATIONS

d to be one of the top three market prospects over
ial trade relations between the two countries con-
by protectionist policies and lack of consumer
ɪltural products.

ates and Korea reached an agreement on Korean
ɔf repeated Korean delays in implementation of the
xports to Korea grew from $25 million in 1988 to
1990. The Korean Government continues to erect
ts affected by a May 1989 agreement. This agree-
ɔort of some 243 agricultural commodities.

rts continues through food safety claims, plant
ustoms classification problems, and anti-import
ɪr 1990, Korea's National Agricultural Cooperatives
istributed an anti-import comic book to 600,000
ɪrged Koreans not to consume imported products
ɪd foods are poisonous and radioactive.

U.S. agricultural imports for December totaled $1.8 billion, down $91 million from November but up $58 million or 3 percent from year ago levels. This marks the third month in a row that imports have increased from year-ago levels, and is consistent with a general longer term trend of rising imports. So far this fiscal year, imports have totaled $5.6 billion, up 4 percent from last year's cumulative figures

Competitive imports for December fell 9 percent from November but are virtually unchanged from last December at $1.35 billion. While the growth of recent months appears to have leveled off somewhat, it still remains above the record setting pace of last year. So far this fiscal year, imports of competitive products total $4.3 billion--up 6 percent above year-ago levels.

Noncompetitive imports g. 13 percent to $454 millio. from last December.

Imports of vegetables in Dec increased 6 percent to $186 r from last year. However, modest overall growth in veg imports masks large increas canned vegetables from Spai 138 percent to $12 million. T crease alone represents 70 perc the total growth in this cat during the month.

Imports of wine and beer were percent to $142 million from ago levels, but were off 31 p from a strong November shc Much of the overall increase from a 24-percent rise in pur from Italy. So far this year, wir beer imports total $556 milli

U.S. Agricultural Imports by Major Product Sector
December 1990 Versus Month-ago and Year-ago

Import Category	Dec 1990	Month Ago	Year Ago	% Change Nov '90 D
	-- Million $ --			
Total competitive	1,354	1,488	1,348	-9%
Fruits, incl. juices	152	121	144	25%
Wines & beer	142	207	135	-31%
Vegetables	186	150	176	24%
Live Animals	116	124	119	2%
Beef & veal	161	158	160	-7%
Dairy products	67	85	84	-21%
Pork	68	82	65	-18%
Total noncompetitive	454	411	402	10%
Coffee & products	162	115	152	40%
Cocoa & products	80	81	61	-2%
Bananas/plantains	77	73	70	5%
Rubber/allied gums	64	69	52	-7%
Spices	20	21	20	-4%
Tea	12	11	12	6%
Total agri. imports	1,808	1,899	1,750	-5%

Source: Commodity Trade Analysis Branch, Economic Research Se U.S. Department of Agriculture, Washington, D.C.

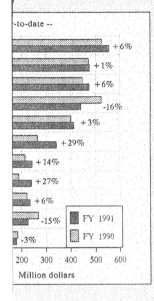

-to-date --

+6%
+1%
+6%
-16%
+3%
+29%
+14%
+27%
+6%
-15%
-3%

FY 1991
FY 1990

| 200 | 300 | 400 | 500 | 600 |

Million dollars

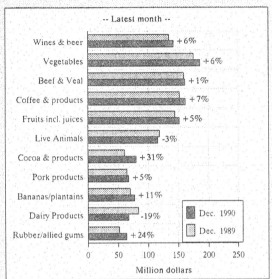

-- Latest month --

Wines & beer	+6%
Vegetables	+6%
Beef & Veal	+1%
Coffee & products	+7%
Fruits incl. juices	+5%
Live Animals	-3%
Cocoa & products	+31%
Pork products	+5%
Bananas/plantains	+11%
Dairy Products	-19%
Rubber/allied gums	+24%

Dec. 1990
Dec. 1989

| 0 | 50 | 100 | 150 | 200 | 250 |

Million dollars

s Summary

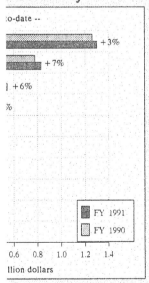

:o-date --

+3%
+7%
+6%
%

FY 1991
FY 1990

| 0.6 | 0.8 | 1.0 | 1.2 | 1.4 |

llion dollars

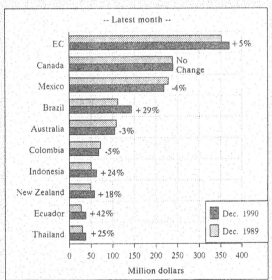

-- Latest month --

EC	+5%
Canada	No Change
Mexico	-4%
Brazil	+29%
Australia	-3%
Colombia	-5%
Indonesia	+24%
New Zealand	+18%
Ecuador	+42%
Thailand	+25%

Dec. 1990
Dec. 1989

| 0 | 50 | 100 | 150 | 200 | 250 | 300 | 350 | 400 |

Million dollars

ted as the change from a year ago.

Financing is a crucial part of every export transaction--and the U.S. Department of Agriculture's Foreign Agricultural Service operates two programs on behalf of the Commodity Credit Corporation (CCC) which are designed to increase the willingness of the private U.S. banking system to extend credit for U.S. agricultural exports.

Under these two programs, which are known as export credit guarantee programs, the U.S. government agrees to pay U.S. exporters--U.S. banks or other financial institutions-- in case a foreign buyer's bank breaks its promise to pay. In this way, USDA reduces the risk involved in selling U.S. agricultural products, and makes both exporters and banks more willing to explore new foreign market opportunities.

USDA itself is not a lender--it merely provides a backup guarantee for the U.S. exporter and the private U.S. financial community in case of nonpayment by foreign banks.

The Two Programs

USDA's two export credit guarantee programs differ primarily in the length of the credit periods they cover. One program covers loans with credit terms of 6 months up to 3 years. This program is known as the Export Credit Guarantee Program (GSM-102). In fiscal 1990, nearly $5 billion in guarantee coverage on U.S. agricultural export sales to 26 different markets was provided under this program. Covered commodities included a broad assortment of U.S. agricultural products, ranging from almonds to feed grains to wheat and wood products.

USDA reduces the risk involved in selling U.S. agricultural products.

The second program operated by USDA covers loans made for over 3 but not more than 10 years. This program is known as the Intermediate Export Credit Guarantee Program (GSM-103). It is used in promoting exports of U.S. agricultural products where particular circumstances make a longer term ap-

propriate. In fisca million in guaran U.S. agricultural e different marke under this program

Eligibility For Gua tion

Every U.S. agricult a foreign buyer is U.S. export cre USDA's guarai generally are made

Top Recipients of GSM Credit Guarantee		
- GSM-102 Allocations - (Million $)		
Country	Fiscal 1991 As of 2/21/91	To Fiscal
Mexico	$1,225	$
Soviet Union	1,000	
Algeria	675	
South Korea	512	
Venezuela	200	
Ecuador	100	
Turkey	80	
Colombia	60	
Pakistan	60	
Trinidad and Tobago	58	
Chile	50	
- GSM-103 Allocations -		
Algeria	$125	
Morocco	98	
Jordan	65	
Sri Lanka	50	
Tunisia	45	
Venezuela	20	
Panama	15	
Mexico	10	
Argentina	2	
Trinidad and Tobago	2	
Ecuador	1	

Source: Foreign Agricultural Service, Export Credits

pects
U.S.
ay be
1ange
make
:isky"
com-
:ers a
ent.

1tions
reign
1ying
1e re-
h the
r At-
bassy
r may
U.S.
Re-
:stina-
antity,
e, the
avail-
bank
it.

1re to
.S. ex-
:xcept
. busi-
s; and
l from

dering
ssue a
cating
yment
com-
t. At
S. ex-
JSDA
S. ex-
erage
1aran-
1e the

Commodities shipped under these programs must be of 100 percent U.S. origin, except the non-agricultural content.

name of the foreign bank which will issue the necessary letter of credit, and the quantity, value, and export period provided in the export credit sale. The guarantee coverage becomes effective only after the U.S. exporter registers the sale with USDA's Foreign Agricultural Service and has shipped under a letter of credit which cannot be revoked. Exporters must maintain documentation on each sale for 3 years after expiration of the coverage provided under the payment guarantee.

What Is Covered by the Guarantee

USDA's guarantee programs can be used to insure payment on 98 percent of the port value of the export item, measured at the U.S. point for overseas shipment, plus a portion of any interest that may be owed. Agricultural commodities or agricultural components shipped under these programs must be of 100-percent U.S. origin, except that non-agricultural content--e.g., vitamins or minerals added to mixed feeds--may be either imported or of U.S. origin. USDA charges a fee for its guarantees.

Who Gets the Money

Since USDA functions not as a lender but only as an underwriter, the U.S. Government is not required to pay out any money under its credit guarantee programs except when a foreign bank does not live up to its commitment to pay. This includes situations where a foreign government's public sector debt is formally rescheduled. Consequently, U.S. Government expenditures for these programs are much smaller than the amounts guaranteed. In the case of a foreign bank's nonpayment, the U.S. Government pays the exporter or his assignee--the assignee is usually a bank or some other type of financial institution in the United States. The U.S. Government then proceeds to collect the overdue amounts from the foreign bank.

For additional information, contact the Commodity Credit Corporation, Operations Division, U.S. Department of Agriculture, Washington, DC 20250-1000, (202) 447-6211.

Uruguay Round Agriculture Negotiations	According to a statement made February 20, t Dunkel, all participants agreed to negotiate to act in each of the three key areas: internal support, ε and to resume negotiation of a sanitary and phytos; of this major impasse, the resumption of the Uru possible. Dunkel scheduled a meeting March 1 to ture. Meetings on other areas of the negotiations s
EC Liberalizes Bovine Semen Imports From the United States	The EC Commission approved a directive conce veterinary certification for the importation of bov The main advantage of the directive is that the sem is limited to December-March, is extended to inc will now be possible to import semen from any pai approved list of U.S. facilities), not just from the However, no implementation date has been includ is authorized through December 31, 1992.
U.S.-EC Enlargement Agreement	Based on calendar year data provided by Spanis chases under the fourth year (1990) of the U.S.- calculated at 129,142 tons of corn and 15,946 ton determined by calculating tenders awarded for rec as recorded shipments of non-grain feed ingre brewer's dregs, and citrus pellets. Once final fig indicated a willingness to tender for the remaining ε
U.S. Bans Imports of Potatoes From Canadian Provinces	On February 6, 1991, following the confirmation o (PVY-N), in Canada, APHIS prohibited entry potatoes originating in the provinces of Princ Brunswick and all potatoes originating in Newf Columbia. Seed potatoes from other locations w from seed potatoes from P.E.I. in 1989 or 1990. from all provinces and territories east of, and incl certificates and treatment of a sprout inhibito. potatoes ($19.5 million) and fresh table potatoes the 1989/90 (July/June) marketing year. Although and peppers, it is most deadly to tobacco. To dat detected in the United States.
ITC Reverses Injury Determination In Pork CVD Case	The International Trade Commission (ITC) issuec its previous positive injury determination in the c ports of fresh, chilled, and frozen pork from Cana to the second remand by a U.S.-Canada Free reviewed the ITC's initial finding in 1990. In rea the legality of the Panel's remand order under Panel issued its first decision challenging the cc determination. In January 1991, after reviewing th the FTA Panel issued a second challenge which Department of Commerce accepts this latest IT Canadian pork, which has been in effect since 198

dent Bush announced on February 5, that Canada will participate in FTA negotia-
with the United States and Mexico. The President notified Congress on that
day of his intent to accept Canadian participation in the negotiations. This
cation is part of the process of negotiating under "fast track" laws and procedures.
²resident had already notified Congress on September 25, 1990, of his intention to
into negotiations with Mexico. Following notification, the relevant Congressional
:nittees - House Ways and Means and Senate Finance -- have 60 legislative days in
1 either Committee can disapprove the use of "fast track" laws and procedures.

to rising red meat prices in Mexico City, the Mexican Government temporarily
:ed import tariffs for swine products from 20 percent to 10 percent. The "seasonal"
s were in effect during the period February 5 to February 25, 1991. On February
he tariffs reverted back to 20 percent. Higher red meat prices were partly at-
ted to high feeder cattle exports to the United States in 1990. Beef shortages
:d consumers to switch to pork, causing increases in swine product prices.

.S. Offical in Taipei has reported that Taiwan's Department of Health has agreed
1plement effective January 1, 1991, an amendment to the AIT-CCNAA Turkey
Memorandum of Understanding regarding phytosanitary "hold-and-test" proce-
s. After completing 10 successive shipments of product without a "violation," sub-
ent shipments of turkey meat from individual U.S. plants will be allowed to enter
an commercial channels immediately upon clearing customs. While these ship-
ts will be randomly sampled, product clearance will not be delayed while awaiting
results. The previous policy required that all shipments of imported turkey be held
fficially controlled warehouses until the Health Department completed product test-
adding unjustified costs and delays (from 7 to 10 working days). It was regarded by
orters as a major obstacle to trade.

1 letter to the U.S. Agricultural Counselor dated January 8, 1991, Philippines
·etary of Agriculture Bancani officially announced the lifting of the ban on fresh
: imports from California which had been put in effect on August 23, 1990 in
onse to press reports of the occurrence of Mediterranean fruit flies (medfly) in the
Angeles area. The announcement followed a series of meetings between the
icultural Counselor and Philippine plant quarantine officials emphasizing the exten-
controls undertaken by APHIS to assure that fruit shipments to all destinations are
of medfly infestation.

le, Paraguay, and the Central African Republic were redesignated as beneficiaries
;eneralized System of Preferences (GSP) benefits. Their redesignation was based
)rogress made in affording internationally recognized worker rights to their workers.
1ibia, formerly ruled by neighboring South Africa, was granted GSP designation in
)gnition of its new status as an independent nation.

Republic of Korea Government (ROKG) has officially announced removal of the
:osanitary ban on pecan imports. Pecans had been "liberalized" in January 1990, but
orts remained banned because of ROKG claims that pecans were host to codling
h.

China Experiments with Suspension of Grain Rationing and Mandatory Production Quotas

China will experiment with grain market reforms in a rural Grain prices will be deregulated, rationing will be abolish shackled from Government production quotas. In a limited the rural economy from most regulation of agricultural inpu and grain prices, the Chinese Government has chosen Guan the pace for reform in the 1990's. Beginning this year, pea all of their grain in the free market or at the Government viously, a stipulated portion of their production was sold t(fixed, low price. After this state quota and on-farm cousu the remiander of the crop (about 39 percent) was sold at Guanghan's urban workers will also lose their grain coup obtain grain at Government subsidized prices and instead w ment. Chinese consumers have been underutilizing the co ners hope that in this grain-rich area, grain production will provide a market incentive.

1991 Swiss Farm Program

The United States Embassy in Bern reports that the Goveri price announcements reflect a movement from indirect, pro direct farm income payments. For livestock producers, f(ment payments will more than double to around $3,620 ani asked to help finance the cost of surplus production. Th supplement payments and on manufacturing subsidies, asi with the Swiss Uruguay Round proposal, is seen as an effo. with those of the EC, in anticipation of more open borders farm budget is currently around $2.1 billion, or 8 percent of

Argentina Eliminates Export Tax on Some Agricultural Products

In an effort to improve farm export earnings, the Governm zero the export taxes paid on live sheep and goats, wool, b by-products. Estimated combined annual sales of these pr ceed $200 million in 1991. Argentina previously reduced t may lower or reduce it on sorghum and corn in the near fut

Materials Available

o The General Agreement on Tariffs and Trade and Wha ture (Revised August 1990)
o The U.S.-Mexico Free Trade Agreement (Fall 1990)
o Comparisons of U.S. and EC Support for Agriculture (R
o Credit Protection for U.S. Agricultural Exporters (Revise
o U.S. Agricultural Exports (December 1990)
o U.S. Agricultural Imports (December 1990)
o The U.S.-EC Enlargement Agreement (January 1991)
o Compilation of Foreign Countries' Methods to Prote Overseas Markets

Trade Policy Updates are prepared monthly by the Trade fice, International Trade Policy, Foreign Agricultural S Agriculture. Requests for copies of Fact Sheets and report the Trade Assistance and Planning Office, 3101 Park Alexandria, VA 22302. Tel: (703) 756-6001. FAX (703) 75

matic
-largest

After enjoying a near monopoly in the South Korean corn market during the last decade, U.S. corn exports could be slashed in half by competition from Chinese sales this year. Already China has reportedly sold over 2.2 million tons, double U.S. sales to date. After 5 years of steady growth, Korea's corn imports are now expected to fall due to competitive feed-quality wheat from Australia, Canada, and the EC substitutes for corn.

s High

EC intervention beef stocks have surpassed 700,000 tons and are expected to exceed the previous all-time record of 800,000 tons by March 31, the end of the marketing year. The EC Commission had set a maximum of 235,000 tons for these stocks but reduced consumption (fallout from the "Mad Cow" disease problem) and slow exports have made holding stocks to that level impossible. Recent efforts to export beef have met with little success. A tender for 80,000 tons to Brazil was scrapped due to lack of interest and the Commission confirmed that no beef has been sold to the Soviet Union in a tender announced in December. Another tender offering 8,000 tons from Ireland, Italy, and the UK was repealed and the Commission estimates that 2,000-3,000 tons had been sold. Two new tenders have been recently opened for a total of 40,000 tons.

port
s Near

The Agricultural Counselor in Tokyo forecasts Japanese beef imports in 1991 at 350,000 tons, 5 percent below the record 365,000 tons believed to have been imported in 1990. As beef imports in Japan are liberalized on April 1, 1991, and tariff rates increase to 70 percent, beef imports are expected to slow down as current high stock levels are drawn down. Japanese beef imports over the next couple of years are expected to continue to grow beyond current levels as market forces begin to operate.

ght's

ners

The drought in Southern California continues to focus the attention of the cotton industry on current and possible future reductions in planted area. California farmers face severe (50-75 percent) cutbacks in water allocations as residential areas increasingly compete for limited supplies. State officials are reportedly encouraging cotton growers and other high water usage crops to idle land. Acreage allocated to cotton (the State's largest cash crop) could be reduced by as much as one-third. Meanwhile, concerns are surfacing overseas with key California San Joaquin Valley (SJV) cotton customers. Some Japanese spinners are worried that upward pressure on SJV prices will force Japan to look increasingly to alternative markets (Australia, China, or the Soviet Union) to satisfy some of its demand for high quality cotton. Japan imports approximately 60,000 bales monthly of California SJV cotton which is highly prized for its strength and uniformity. Currently, California SJV is being sold at about $.93 per pound compared with $.86 per pound for comparable Chinese growths. Spinners expect the price spread to widen if drought relief is not forthcoming.

ublic Buys
<

CCC has made a direct sale of 306.2 tons of nonfat dry milk for March shipment to the Dominican Republic at a price of $1,400 per ton. The sale is the first direct sale of nonfat dry milk since fiscal 1988. Other direct sales this year have been made for 8,000 metric tons of butter oil, bringing total direct sales to $10.9 million for fiscal 1991.

es To
r Exports

Trade sources report a total of 300,000 tons of broiler meat exported from Brazil in 1990. This is a 23-percent increase over 1989 exports. Brazil ranks third in world trade for broilers, preceded by France (370,000 tons) and the United States (493,000 tons). The increase of exports reflects new shipments for Cuba, the Soviet Union, and Japan.

Chilean Fruit Producers To Press Legal Action for 1989 Poisoned Fruit Incident

Press accounts in Chile have been detailing the fruit growers' a
go forward with legal action to claim indemnification for their l
U.S. Food and Drug Administration (FDA) embargo on Chile
The action followed the discovery by FDA of cyanide-con
Chilean fruit industry plans to bring charges against the Unite
Philadelphia on February 26, 1991. The Chilean fruit industry
for court costs which could reach between $2 and $4 million.

Egyptian Cigarette Sales To USSR Bode Well for U.S. Tobacco Growers

Eastern Tobacco Company, Egypt's state monopoly for cigaret
for new markets to maintain production levels and to earn fo
reports state that 200 million cigarettes, valued at $5 million, v
under their annual barter agreement. Eastern is also consideri
high-quality cigarette containing U.S. tobacco. The new cigare
the upscale domestic market and the export market. If success
to Egypt could rise.

Brazil Revises Import Tariffs for Agricultural Products

The Government of Brazil has announced implementation of i
The objective is to achieve an average tariff of 20 percent by
ranging from zero to 40 percent. Brazil also elaborated on ste
toward import liberalization, including elimination of nontariff
port licenses, quotas, and the prohibited products list. The g
provide the Brazilian economy with "stable protection" throu
porary tariffs for the next 4 years. The aim is to stimulate dor
foreign competition.

U.S. Broiler Exports for 1991 Revised Downward

The estimate of U.S. broiler exports for 1991 has been
517,000 tons to 465,000 tons. This reflects a steady rate of e
destinations, with a drop in exports to the Soviet Union. Ex
are expected to decline due to continuing hard currency s
credit guarantees. The $25 million extended under the U.
Soviet poultry purchases has been exhausted.

EC Increases Export Refunds for Butter to The Soviet Union

The EC Commission, on January 25, announced that the Dai
tee increased export refunds for butter destined for the
ECU/100kg ($240) to 212 ECU/100Kg ($292). The refund v
presented for export to the USSR, including butter from inte
ing to a commission source, the committee increased the refu
for EC traders to supply 200,000 tons of butter to the Soviet
announced to the International Dairy Arrangement (IDA) c
refund level was arrived at on the basis of a $1000/ton FOB pr

Venezuela Likely To Import U.S. Rice

For the first time, Venezuela may import U.S. rice due to incr
tion and low stocks. Venezuela produces about 370,000 tons
covered most of total domestic consumption during the last te.
favorable prices. domestic demand has increased more than su
lead to imports of 100,000 tons before the end of February.
pected to turn to Colombia, but reduced supplies in that cou
an attractive alternative.

s Some U.S.
s
On January 23, Norwegian Plant Inspection authorities inspected and then withdrew from the market several pallets of U.S. pears after Norwegian laboratories reported the existence of dead and live San Jose Scale, a fruit pest. Norway has a zero tolerance for the pest. The inspections were made at the retail level after the shipments had already cleared customs/quarantine inspection. On January 25, Norwegian inspection authorities decided to re-inspect all pear stocks currently stored in warehouses.

ces Import
for Livestock
ucts
Effective January 1, 1991, 10 livestock and 35 fish products were granted automatic approval for importation. Although the immediate positive impact on U.S. exports is not expected to be dramatic, this development is viewed as a step in the right direction. Examples of the products liberalized include lamb, pork offal, venison meat, crab meat, and processed turkey meat.

ports
ecrease
Following the December freeze in California, total U.S. citrus exports in 1990/91 are now forecast at 870,000 tons, 6 percent below the previous season's shipments. A significant reduction in fresh orange exports shipments accounts for most of the decrease. The 1990/91 California orange crop is now forecast at 851,000 tons, down from 2.4 million tons last year. Total U.S. fresh orange exports in 1990/91 are forecast at 260,000 tons, down almost 50 percent from last year and the lowest export figure for U.S. oranges since 1970. The decline in orange shipments will be partially offset by an anticipated increase in U.S. grapefruit exports based on a sharp increase in Florida grapefruit output. Total U.S. grapefruit exports in 1990/91 are forecast at 475,000 tons, 66 percent above the previous season's shipments and about the same as the 1988/89 record volume.

s Imported
Vith Captan
Effective January 14, 1991, imported strawberries containing any trace of the fungicide Captan will not be allowed entry into Australia. Both Environmental Protection Agency (EPA) and the Codex Alimentarius have established tolerance levels for Captan, and the fungicide is used by California strawberry growers based on local rainfall conditions. Although most U.S. shipments tested thus far have been found free of Captan, the U.S. industry is concerned both about the scientific basis for the ban and the potential effect on quality from delays in testing upon arrival in Australia.

orts to
ue To Soar
Korea is the number three U.S. beef market for the second year in a row after several years of only token beef imports. U.S. census data through November 1990 put U.S. beef exports to Korea at $102 million, 28 percent higher than the record 1989 export total of $80 million. The U.S. market share in Korea during 1990 stood at 32 percent of total beef imports and 98 percent of high-quality beef (HQB) imports, compared to 24 percent and 91 percent, respectively, in 1989.

For more information, contact Emiko Miyasaka, (202) 382-9054

Annual Performance Indicators Including Fiscal 1991 Forecasts

	December 1989	1990	Change	Year to Date Oct–Dec 1989	Oct–Dec 1990	Change	Fiscal Year 1990	1991(f)	Change
	--Bil.$--			--Bil.$--			--Bil.$--		
s 1/	1.535	0.958	-38%	4.389	3.131	-29%	16.019	13.8	-14%
	0.362	0.179	-51%	1.067	0.682	-36%	4.224	3.1	-27%
	0.015	0.015	3%	0.063	0.043	-31%	0.202	0.2	-1%
	0.083	0.077	-7%	0.263	0.236	-11%	0.830	0.8	-4%
s 2/	0.821	0.448	-45%	2.294	1.359	-41%	7.962	7.0	-12%
	0.740	0.378	-49%	2.036	1.132	-44%	6.929	6.0	-13%
)dders	0.174	0.144	-17%	0.443	0.470	6%	1.812	NA	NA
oducts	0.624	0.507	-19%	1.893	1.463	-23%	6.253	6.2	-1%
	0.407	0.343	-16%	1.326	0.935	-29%	3.939	3.9	-1%
eal	0.113	0.079	-30%	0.247	0.232	-6%	0.990	1.1	11%
il	0.024	0.004	-83%	0.067	0.041	-39%	0.339	0.3	-12%
:table oils	0.033	0.034	3%	0.095	0.096	1%	0.394	NA	NA
ducts	0.449	0.459	2%	1.363	1.453	7%	5.418	5.5	2%
	0.157	0.188	20%	0.519	0.611	18%	2.181	NA	NA
kins	0.145	0.120	-17%	0.419	0.376	-10%	0.468	NA	NA
icts	0.061	0.072	18%	0.190	0.244	28%	0.856	0.9	5%
eat	0.044	0.052	18%	0.136	0.177	30%	0.624	NA	NA
ts	0.033	0.020	-40%	0.090	0.064	-30%	0.342	0.5	46%
products	0.309	0.466	51%	1.138	1.591	40%	5.154	5.5	7%
red tobacco	0.113	0.193	71%	0.399	0.481	21%	1.373	1.4	2%
ers	0.252	0.284	13%	0.614	0.693	13%	2.719	2.7	-1%
s	0.080	0.071	-12%	0.162	0.172	6%	0.580	0.6	3%
ical products	0.109	0.131	20%	0.350	0.445	27%	1.401	1.4	0%
ort value	3.565	3.161	-11%	10.587	9.736	-8%	40.118	38.5	-4%
s 1/	11.009	7.219	-34%	31.627	23.201	-27%	113.555	NA	NA
	2.225	1.535	-31%	6.559	5.910	-10%	28.095	27.5	-2%
ur	0.071	0.089	25%	0.272	0.224	-18%	0.88	1.2	36%
	0.263	0.293	12%	0.807	0.839	4%	2.502	2.4	-4%
is 2/	7.273	4.310	-41%	20.768	12.804	-38%	69.031	59.8	-13%
	6.563	3.598	-45%	18.457	10.607	-43%	59.878	51.8	-13%
odders	1.033	0.837	-19%	2.719	2.836	4%	11.065	11.9	8%
roducts	2.504	2.023	-19%	7.549	5.610	-26%	24.046	NA	NA
	1.790	1.502	-16%	5.889	4.020	-32%	17.217	16.6	-4%
eal	0.519	0.380	-27%	1.102	1.096	-1%	4.558	5.0	10%
il	0.051	0.006	-88%	0.142	0.064	-55%	0.614	0.6	-2%
:table oils	0.058	0.055	-5%	0.159	0.144	-9%	0.618	NA	NA
ducts 3/	0.212	0.190	-11%	0.644	0.544	-16%	2.381	NA	NA
	0.058	0.054	-6%	0.191	0.178	-7%	0.676	0.7	4%
icts 3/	0.043	0.045	5%	0.127	0.161	27%	0.564	NA	NA
eat	0.042	0.045	7%	0.126	0.159	26%	0.56	0.6	7%
ts 3/	0.021	0.014	-34%	0.057	0.041	-28%	0.214	NA	NA
products 3/	0.281	0.433	54%	1.004	1.420	41%	4.565	5.0	10%
red tobacco	0.020	0.031	59%	0.068	0.074	9%	0.22	0.2	-9%
ers	0.154	0.171	11%	0.385	0.416	8%	1.703	1.6	-6%
s	0.048	0.049	3%	0.119	0.105	-12%	0.578	NA	NA
ical products 3/	0.056	0.086	53%	0.215	0.284	32%	0.921	NA	NA
ort volume 3/	14.347	10.261	-28%	41.795	31.856	-24%	148.749	139.5	-6%

aila lc.

ilses, corn gluten feed, and neal.

rn, oats, barley, rye, and sorghun.

ly those items neasured in netric tons.

orecasts are taken from "Outlook for U.S. Agricultural Exports", Nov. 27, 1990.

U.S. Agricultural Export Value by Region
Monthly and Annual Performance Indicators

	December 1989	December 1990	
	--Bil.$--		Chg
Western Europe	0.743	0.805	8%
European Community 1/	0.705	0.757	7%
Other Western Europe	0.038	0.048	27%
Eastern Europe	0.020	0.028	43%
Soviet Union	0.384	0.052	-87%
Asia	1.621	1.370	-15%
Japan	0.673	0.706	5%
China	0.090	0.039	-57%
Other East Asia	0.510	0.390	-24%
Taiwan	0.234	0.138	-41%
South Korea	0.225	0.187	-17%
Hong Kong	0.051	0.064	25%
Other Asia	0.129	0.116	-10%
Pakistan	0.051	0.002	-96%
Philippines	0.011	0.033	196%
Middle East	0.219	0.119	-45%
Iraq	0.088	0.000	-100%
Saudi Arabia	0.053	0.060	13%
Africa	0.167	0.109	-34%
North Africa	0.132	0.078	-41%
Egypt	0.052	0.040	-22%
Algeria	0.030	0.021	-30%
Sub Saharan Africa	0.035	0.031	-10%
Latin America	0.584	0.755	29%
Mexico	0.196	0.189	-4%
Other Latin America	0.215	0.264	23%
Brazil	0.012	0.057	393%
Venezuela	0.029	0.026	-12%
Canada*	0.172	0.301	75%
Oceania	0.032	0.029	-10
World Total	3.565	3.161	-11

*Prior to 1990, it is estimated that U.S. agricultural exports
Bureau of the Census were understated. Data prior to Janua
1/ Excluding East Germany prior to fiscal 1991; including

Weekly Quotations for
Selected International Prices 1/

Dollars per metric ton	Week of 2/19/91
Wheat (c.i.f. Rotterdam) 2/	
Canadian No. 1 CWRS 13.5%	144
U.S. No. 2 DNS 14 %	NQ
U.S. No. 2 SRW	131
U.S. No. 3 HAD	151
Canadian No. 1 durum	155
Feed Grains (c.i.f. Rotterdam) 2/	
U.S. No. 3 yellow corn	126
Soybeans and Meal (c.i.f. Rotterdam) 2/	
U.S. No. 2 yellow soybeans	242
U.S. 44 % soybean meal	NQ
Brazil 48 % soy pellets	204
U.S. Farm Prices 3/ 4/	
Wheat	89
Barley	82
Corn	89
Sorghum	86
Broiler 5/	1,146
Soybeans 6/	211
EC Import Levies	
Common wheat	140
Durum wheat	146
Barley	118
Corn	102
Sorghum	109
Broilers	NA
EC Intervention Prices 7/	
Premium Wheat	124
Common Wheat	122
Feed Wheat	115
Maize	122
Barley	115
Sorghum	NA
Broilers	NA
EC Export Restitution (subsidies) 8/	
Common wheat	86
Barley	78
Broilers	NA

NQ = No quote. NA = Not available. Note: Changes in dollar value of EC imp restitutions may be the result of changes in $/ECU exchange rates.

1/ Mid-week quote. 2/ Asking price in dollars for imported grain and soybeans delivery. 3/ Five-day moving average. 4/ Target price for current market wheat, $147; barley, $108; corn, $107; sorghum, $103. 5/ Composite 12-city we sales to be delivered to first receiver. 6/ Central Illinois processors bid to arrive. intervention price plus full value of monthly increments. 8/ Figures represent res listed dates; (*) denotes no award given since the previous month.

FAS.Circulars:
Market Information For
Agricultural Exporters

As an agricultural exporter, you need timely, reliable information on changing consumer preferences, needs of foreign buyers, and the supply and demand situation in countries around the world.

The Foreign Agricultural Service can provide that information in its commodity circulars.

World agricultural information and updates on·special FAS export services for the food and agricultural trade all are available in these periodic circulars.

For a sample copy of these reports—which can supply you with the information you need to make sound business decisions—check the box indicated, fill out the address form, and mail it today.

To subscribe: Indicate which publications you want. Send a check for the tot payable to the Foreign Agricultural Service. Only checks on U.S. banks, cas or international money orders will be accepted. NO REFUNDS CAN BE MA
Mail this form to: Foreign Agricultural Service
Information Division
Room 4644-S
U.S. Department of Agriculture
Washington, D.C. 20250-1000

No. of Subscriptions		Subsc
		Dome
_____ 10002	Agricultural Trade Highlights (12 issues)	$17.C
_____ 10022	World Cocoa Situation (2 issues)	6.C
_____ 10003	World Coffee Situation (3 issues)	5.C
_____ 10004	World Cotton Situation (12 issues)	26.C
	Dairy, Livestock & Poultry:	
_____ 10005	Dairy, Livestock & Poultry: U.S. Trade & Prospects (12 issues)	32.C
_____ 10006	Dairy Monthly Imports (12 issues)	17.C
_____ 10007	World Dairy Situation (2 issues)	5.C
_____ 10008	World Livestock Situation (2 issues); World Poultry Situation (2 issues)	10.C
_____ 10009	All 30 Dairy, Livestock & Poultry Reports	53.C
	Grain:	
_____ 10010	World Grain Situation & Outlook (12 issues)	23.C
_____ 10011	Export Markets for U.S. Grain & Products (12 issues)	24.0
_____ 10014	All 24 Grain Reports	43.0
_____ 10015	Horticultural Products Review (12 issues)	23.0
_____ 10016	World Oilseed Situation & Market Highlights (12 issues)	32.0
_____ 10017	U.S. Seed Exports (4 issues)	16.0
_____ 10018	World Sugar and Molasses Situation & Outlook; World Honey Situation (3 issues)	8.0
_____ 10019	World Tea Situation; U.S. Spice Trade; U.S. Essential Oil Trade (3 issues)	7.0
_____ 10020	World Tobacco Situation (12 issues)	29.0
_____ 10021	World Agricultural Production (12 issues)	29.0
_____ 10023	Wood Products: International Trade and Foreign Markets (4 issues)	14.0

Total Reports Ordered   **Total Subscription Pr**

☐ Please send me a sample copy.

Enclosed is my Check for $ _____ Made Payable to Foreign Agricultur

Name (Last, first, middle initial)

Organization or Firm

Street or P.O. Box Number

City   St

Country   Phone

Important Notice to Readers --

Agricultural Trade Highlights is available on a
fee is $17 in the United States or $36 for for
check, payable to the Foreign Agricultural
USDA, Room 4644-South Building, Washingt
on U.S. banks, or international money orders
MADE.

This publication is a product of the Trade an
Agricultural Service, U.S. Department of
Washington, D.C. 20250-1000. Questions on
directed to Mike Dwyer at (202) 382-1294.